Date: 8/30/23

PA T5-ACZ-617

**3650 Summit Boulevard
West Palm Beach, FL 33406**

Published in 2022 by Rosen Publishing
29 East 21st Street, New York, NY 10010

Copyright © 2021 Alix Wood Books

Adaptations to North American edition © 2021
by Rosen Publishing

All rights reserved. No part of this book may be reproduced in any form without permission in writing from the publisher, except by a reviewer.

Produced for Rosen Publishing by Alix Wood Books
Designed and Illustrated by Alix Wood
Editor: Eloise Macgregor
Consultant: Kate Spencer, Professor of Environmental Geochemistry

Cataloging-in-Publication Data
Names: Wood, Alix.
Title: Get hands-on with fossils! / Alix Wood.
Description: New York : PowerKids Press, 2022. | Series: Hands-on geology | Includes glossary and index.
Identifiers: ISBN 9781725331235 (pbk.) | ISBN 9781725331259 (library bound) | ISBN 9781725331242 (6 pack) | ISBN 9781725331266 (ebook)
Subjects: LCSH: Fossils--Juvenile literature.
Classification: LCC QE714.5 W66 2022 | DDC 560--dc23

Photo credits:
Cover, 3, 4, 6 all except 6 middle inset, 8, 12 bottom, 14, 15, 20 all except top, 23, 24 © Adobe Stock Images; 6 middle inset @ Denali National Park & Preserve, Alaska (public domain); 7 © Havardtl (public domain); 12 middle © Desert Museum, Saltillo (public domain); 20 top © needpix.com; all other photographic images are in the public domain

Illustrations © Alix Wood

All rights reserved. No part of this book may be reproduced in any form without permission from the publisher, except by reviewer.

Printed in the United States of America

CPSIA Compliance Information: Batch #CSPK22. For Further Information contact Rosen Publishing, New York, New York at 1-800-237-9932.

Contents

What Are Fossils? 4

Different Types of Fossils 6

The Perfect Conditions 8

How Does Sediment Turn to Rock? 10

Whole Animal Fossils 12

More Amazing Fossils 14

Where Can You Find Fossils? 16

How the Experts Dig Up Fossils 18

Fossil Identification 20

Travel Through Time 22

How Old Is My Fossil? 24

Using Maps to Help Find Fossils 26

Sharing the Knowledge 28

Glossary 30

Further Information 31

Index 32

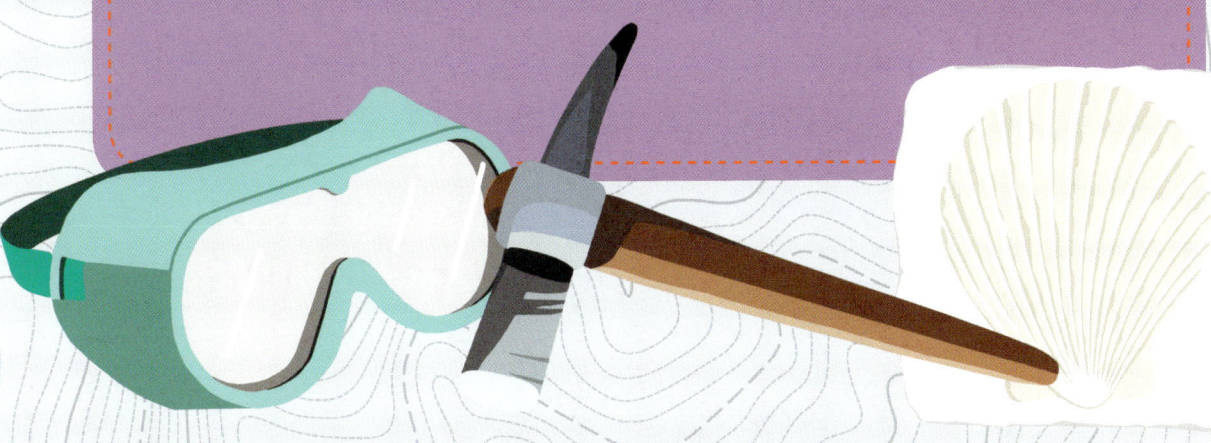

What Are Fossils?

Fossils are the remains or traces of plants and animals that lived long ago. If you have a rock collection, look closely. You may find tiny fossils, millions of years old, embedded in some of them. The word fossil comes from the Latin word *fossilis*, which means "dug up."

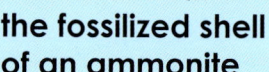

the fossilized shell of an ammonite

Most of the fossils that we find come from areas that were once underwater. A type of rock that forms underwater, **sedimentary rock**, creates the perfect conditions for forming fossils. That is why most fossils are of sea creatures, or animals whose bodies fell into water.

How Fossils Form

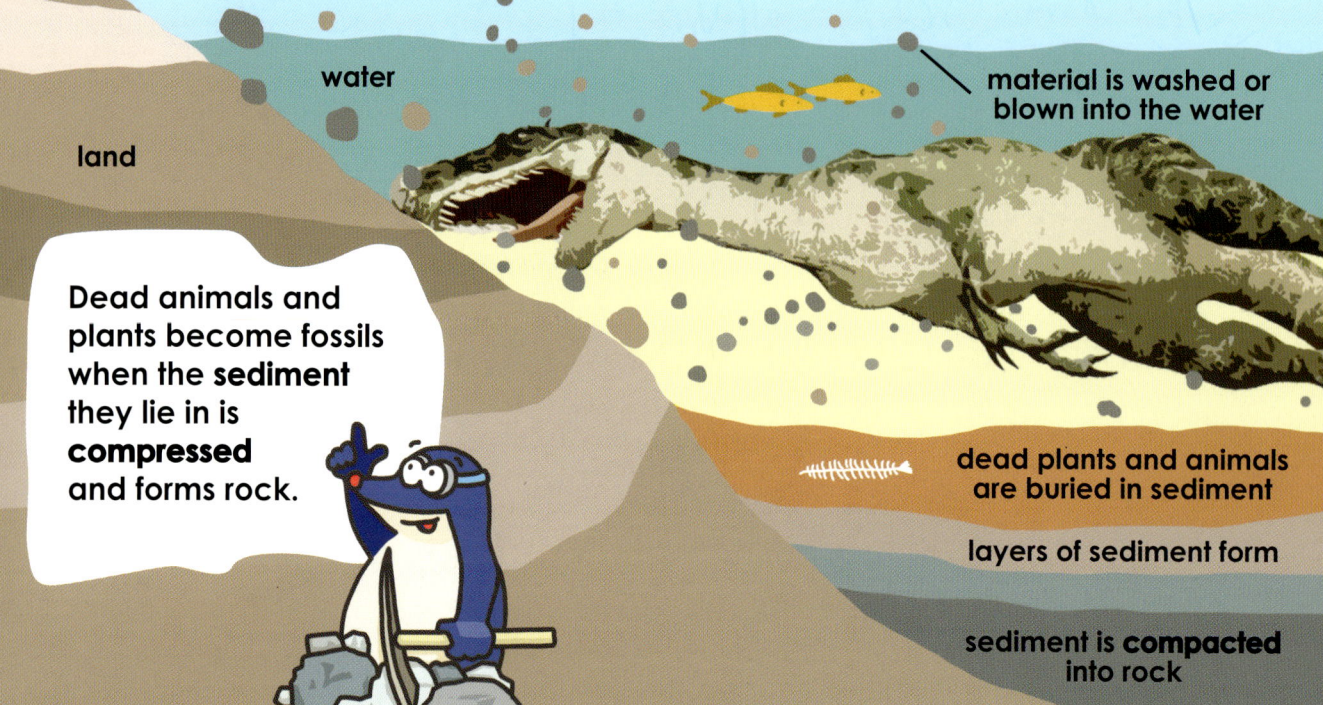

- water
- land
- material is washed or blown into the water
- dead plants and animals are buried in sediment
- layers of sediment form
- sediment is **compacted** into rock

Dead animals and plants become fossils when the **sediment** they lie in is **compressed** and forms rock.

Why Study Fossils?

Fossils give scientists clues about the past. People who study fossils are called **paleontologists**. "Paleo" means ancient, and "ontology" is the study of existence. Paleontologists' discoveries have helped them piece together what Earth would have been like millions of years ago. Fossils help show what **extinct** animals looked like, where they lived, and why they may have become extinct. They also give clues about what Earth looked like long ago.

Think About This...

Long ago, Earth looked very different. Oceans covered areas that are now land. Some **continents** were joined together that now have an ocean between them. How do you think fossils helped scientists work that out?

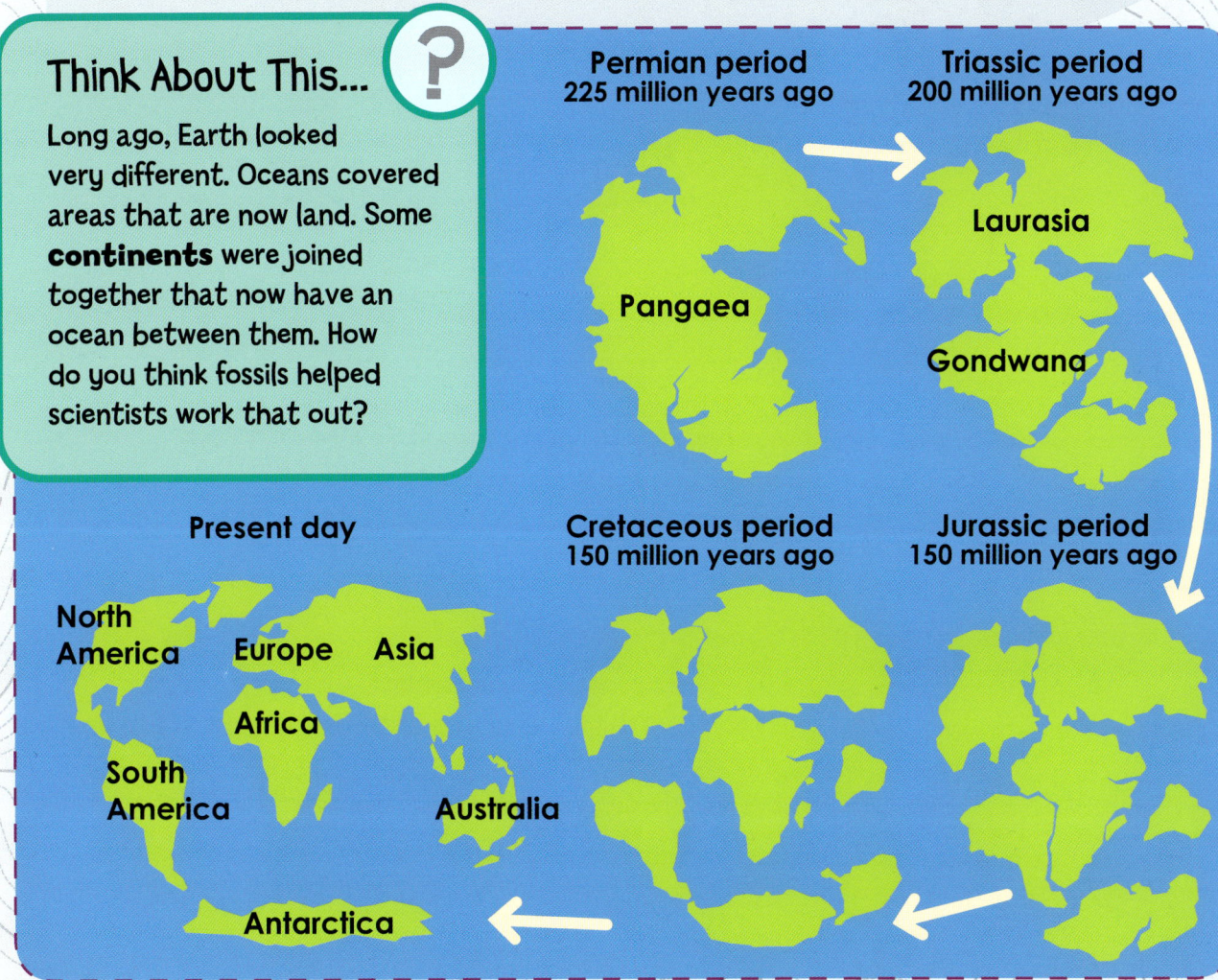

HANDS-ON Make a Continent Jigsaw

You Will Need:
- a map or globe
- thin paper
- pencil
- scissors

Trace the outlines of the present-day continents using a map or globe. Carefully cut them out. See how well you can fit the continents together. Do any still fit quite well? Can you make something that looks a little like Pangaea? Why do you think some continents might not fit well together anymore?

Different Types of Fossils

Animal and plant remains can turn into fossils in different ways. There are two main types of fossils—body fossils and trace fossils.

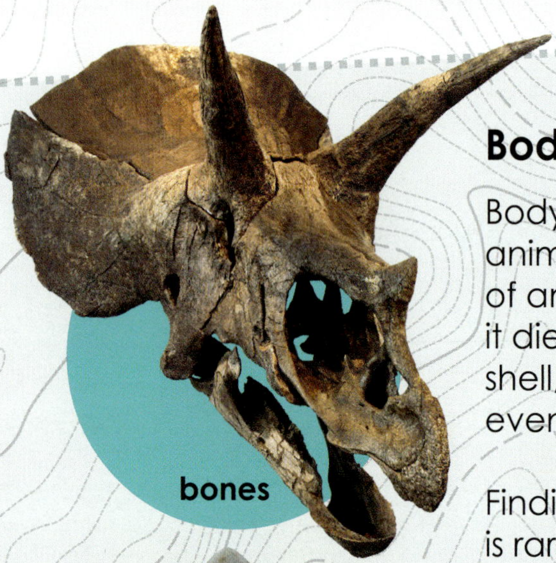

Body Fossils

Body fossils are the remains of plants or animals that were once living. The soft parts of an animal's body usually rot away once it dies. But the hard parts—the teeth, claws, shell, and bones—might be preserved and eventually harden into rock.

Finding a complete dinosaur skeleton is rare. Usually, the bones have been scattered either by animals, the weather, or flowing water. The skulls, being hollow and lightweight, have often been crushed or are missing.

Teeth are covered in a substance called enamel that is harder than bone. Sometimes the teeth are the only part of a species of dinosaur that is ever found. Some dinosaurs, such as *Megalosaurus*, used to shed their teeth regularly and grow new ones, so fossilized *Megalosaurus* teeth are quite common.

bones

teeth

leaves

shells

Stranger types of body fossils include fossilized poop (known as a **coprolite**), skin imprints, and eggs!

poop   skin   egg

Trace Fossils

Trace fossils are fossils of signs that a plant or animal lived, rather than fossils of the animal or plant itself. They are fascinating. Holes near bird tracks show birds used their beaks to find food. A burrow in the same rock may show what insect the birds were looking for!

These dinosaur tracks are a trace fossil.

Think About This...

Fossilization is so unlikely that less than one-tenth of one percent of animal species that ever lived have become fossils! How many do you think have actually been found?

BE A PALEONTOLOGIST
Make Your Own Trace Fossil

You Will Need:
- a cup of flour
- a cup of salt
- a cup of water
- bowl
- spoon
- greased baking sheet
- toy plastic dinosaur

How to Make Footprints:

Put half the salt and all the flour into a bowl and mix together. Mix in the water a little at a time. Gradually add more salt until the mixture is not too sticky and feels like dough.

Roll the dough into a ball. Flatten it until around an inch (2.5 cm) thick and place it on the baking sheet. Dip the dinosaur's feet in flour, then press the feet into the dough. Leave to dry for a couple of days, or bake for 20 minutes at 350 degrees Fahrenheit.

The Geology:

Paleontologists can tell all kinds of things from dinosaur footprints. They can tell the speed the dinosaur ran, its size, the number of legs it had, and if the dinosaur traveled in groups.

The Perfect Conditions

Not every animal or plant that dies is turned into a fossil. The conditions have to be just right. Most fossils are formed by a process known as "mold and cast." When an animal or plant dies in sediment, its body is dissolved by water seeping through the rock. As it dissolves, it leaves a hollow mold where it was. **Minerals** in the water fill the mold and replace the bone. This creates a rock **replica**, a little like a cast statue, of the original skeleton.

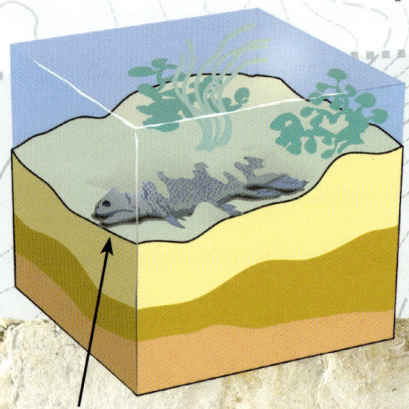

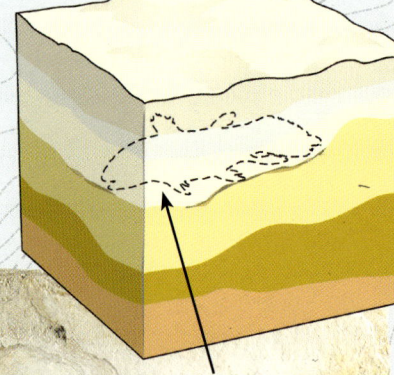

A fish dies and its body falls to the bottom of the water. After a while only its skeleton is left.

The bones of the skeleton create a hollow in the sediment.

The buried bones gradually dissolve, replaced by minerals that fill the hollow.

It can take millions of years for minerals in groundwater to fill the mold. Eventually, the skeleton becomes solid rock. The fossil will remain underground until either the surrounding rock is worn away and exposes the fossil, or it is dug up by fossil hunters.

Think About This...

Why do you think fossilized worms are very rare?

BE A PALEONTOLOGIST
Make a Mold and Cast Fossil

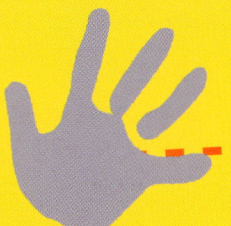

You Will Need:

- small plastic or foil container
- modeling clay
- a shell (or a plastic dinosaur)
- petroleum jelly
- plaster of Paris
- a bowl and mixing spoon
- water
- rubber gloves, eye protection, and face mask

How to Make Your Fossil:

Knead the modeling clay until soft. Place a 1-inch (2.5 cm) layer of clay in the bottom of a small container. Smear your shell in petroleum jelly. This makes it easier to remove the shell once the plaster has set. Press the shell into the clay, then remove it carefully so the print doesn't smudge. If the shell won't come out, hold an edge and gently rock the shell back and forth.

Put on eye protection, gloves, and a face mask. Plaster of Paris can irritate your eyes, skin, and lungs. Measure the plaster into a bowl, following the instructions on the packet. Mix enough plaster to fill your mold and cover the clay. Using a spoon, mix the plaster with water until it is quite runny. Spoon the mixture into the mold. Smooth the plaster to form a flat surface and then let it dry for around 24 hours.

Turn the container upside down. Gently press out the mold. Carefully peel the clay from the plaster. Now you have your very own fossil! Keep it safe - you'll use it again later.

The Geology:

The modeling clay in this activity acts like the riverbed.

Pressing the shell into the clay represents the dead animal making a hollow in the sediment. The animal gradually decays, leaving a mold of its original shape.

Removing the shell and filling the mold with plaster represents the minerals replacing the animal's body and forming the fossil.

How Does Sediment Turn to Rock?

Sediment is material—such as sand, minerals, and the remains of plants and animals—that is washed, blown, or moved by ice to areas such as riverbeds. How does sediment turn into rock? When sediment is compacted and **cemented** by great pressure, any liquid or gaps that existed in the sediment are pressed out. Sediment is gradually compressed so much that it becomes solid.

extreme pressure

This process of turning sediment to rock is known as **lithification**. *Lithos* means "rock" in Greek. Try the experiments on these pages to understand how lithification happens, and make you very own rock!

HANDS-ON Make a Jar of Sediment

You will need:
- dirt, soil, leaves, sand, and pebbles
- a large jar with a lid
- some water
- a small plastic dinosaur

First, go outside and collect lots of different materials that might be found in sediment. For example, gather leaves, compost, soil, clay, small rocks, and sand.

Fill a jar three-quarters full of water. Put most of your collected dirt into the jar. Put on the lid and shake the jar. You should see the water turn brown as the material mixes in with the water. As the dirt starts to settle, try to guess which materials will sink and which will float to the top.

Place your plastic dinosaur into the jar and watch where it settles. Does it sink below any of the layers? What happens if you sprinkle the rest of the mixture on top?

There are two processes that turn sediment into rock.

Compaction
The loose particles in sediment are squashed by their own weight and the weight above them. Eventually, there is little or no empty space left between each particle.

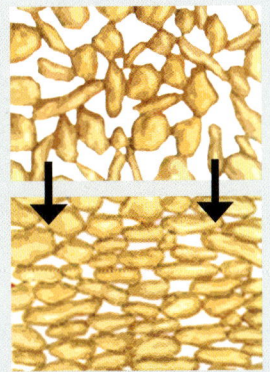

Cementation
Minerals crystallize in the spaces between particles and hold them tightly together.

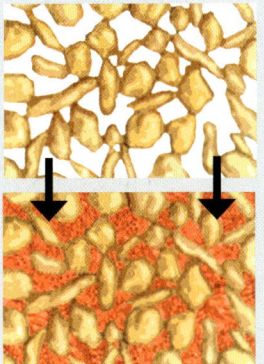

BE A PALEONTOLOGIST
Try Compaction and Cementation

You Will Need:

- sand
- water
- plaster of Paris
- scissors
- two small yogurt containers
- an old bowl and tablespoon
- eye protection, gloves, and face mask

adult help needed

How to Make Your Own Rock:

Dampen some sand with water. Half fill a yogurt container with the sand and press it down very firmly. Carefully cut away the plastic container. You may need an adult to help you. Leave the compacted sand "rock" to dry.

Now repeat the same experiment, but this time instead of just using damp sand, mix in some "cement." Put on eye protection, gloves, and a face mask, as plaster of Paris can irritate your eyes, skin, and lungs. In an old bowl, mix one tablespoon of plaster of Paris to four tablespoons of damp sand. Firmly press the sand into the yogurt container. Then cut away the container and leave your "rock" to dry.

Which process made the hardest "rock" from your sand, compaction or cementation?

The Geology:

Some sediment can be compacted to form rock. Sand and coarse-grained sediment needs a natural "cement" made from minerals to bind it. The chemicals that act as cement are found in **groundwater**. They are usually silica, calcium carbonate, or iron **compounds**.

11

Whole Animal Fossils

Not all fossils are found in sedimentary rock. Usually, when an animal dies, **bacteria** eats away at the soft parts of the body. However, bacteria do not like very cold or dry conditions. Animals that die in a desert cave or are quickly frozen in ice may be fossilized whole.

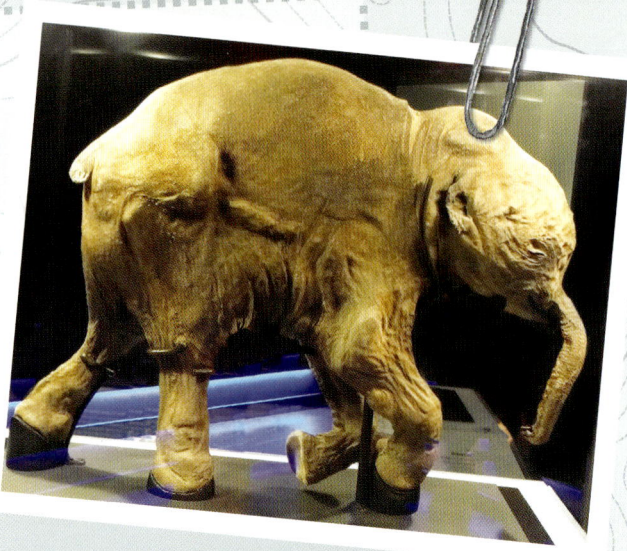

Whole animal fossils, like this fish, have been found in deserts, their bodies preserved by the dry air.

This baby woolly mammoth fossil was buried in mud and clay that quickly froze, preserving it. The stomach still had traces of its mother's milk. The mammoth died around 42,000 years ago!

Think About This...

What could paleontologists learn from a whole animal fossil that they couldn't tell from just bones and teeth?

Trapped!

When an animal becomes trapped in tree **resin**, its whole body may get preserved. When an insect lands on some sticky tree resin, it can become stuck. Over time, more resin falls on top of it. Over millions of years the resin hardens and changes into a hard material called amber.

Whole dead animals and plants can become preserved in **paraffin**, and in a decaying plant matter known as peat too.

a spider trapped in amber

12

BE A PALEONTOLOGIST
Make an Amber Fossil

You Will Need:

- clear nail polish
- modeling clay
- yellow and red food coloring
- some newspaper
- a small dead insect (or plastic toy insect)

adult help needed

Windowsills or wood piles are a good place to find a dead insect. Never use an insect you think might be alive. If you can't find a dead insect, use a plastic one instead.

The Geology:

Nature is very good at getting rid of waste. Animals and plants **decompose** when they die. How? Bacteria break down the soft tissues. Some types of animals and birds, known as scavengers, will eat dead animals. Certain insects eat plant and animal waste, too. Weather and erosion can break down any bones and teeth that are left.

It is amazing that any whole body fossils have been found!

How to Make Your Fossil:

Roll a small ball of modeling clay. Press your thumb in the middle to make a hole large enough to fit your dead or toy insect. This will be your mold.

Ask an adult to help you, as nail polish and food color will stain. Cover a table with newspaper. Carefully open the nail polish. Put a few drops of yellow and one drop of red food coloring into the polish. Screw the lid on tightly and shake the mixture. It should now look amber-colored.

Pour a small amount of nail polish into the bottom of the clay mold you made. Place the insect in the hole.

Wait around 15 minutes for the polish to dry so it glues the insect in place. Then gradually add more layers of polish, a little at a time. Let it dry between each layer. When the insect is fully covered, leave your mold to dry for a few hours. When it is completely dry, peel the modeling clay away from your "amber" fossil.

13

More Amazing Fossils

Paleontologists can answer a lot of questions about ancient times by examining puzzling fossils. For example, what are the smooth, strange rocks sometimes found near dinosaur skeletons? Was the Arizona desert once really a forest?

A Fossil Forest

All plants, even huge trees, can become fossils. **Petrified** wood is wood that has turned to stone. Just as with animal bones, minerals in water can preserve trees buried in **volcanic** ash or sediment, replacing the wood to form fossils. If you look closely at a piece of petrified wood you might see tree rings, bark, and maybe even insects that had burrowed into the wood.

Huge chunks of petrified trees can be found at the Petrified Forest National Park in Arizona. The fossils are an ancient type of conifer tree common when dinosaurs roamed the Earth. Some of the giant trees are thought to have been over 164 feet (50 m) tall!

Different minerals create different-colored fossils. Iron has turned this wood red and orange. Manganese creates blue, purple, and black fossils. Copper can turn them green.

Using Rocks As Teeth!

Some dinosaurs swallowed rocks to help them digest their food. As the dinosaurs did not have grinding teeth, they used the rocks to grind food in a special area of their stomachs. These smoothed stones, known as **gastroliths**, have been found in or near dinosaur fossils.

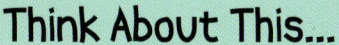

Think About This...
Can you think of any modern animals that use rocks to digest their food?

BE A PALEONTOLOGIST
Gastroliths? Examine the Evidence

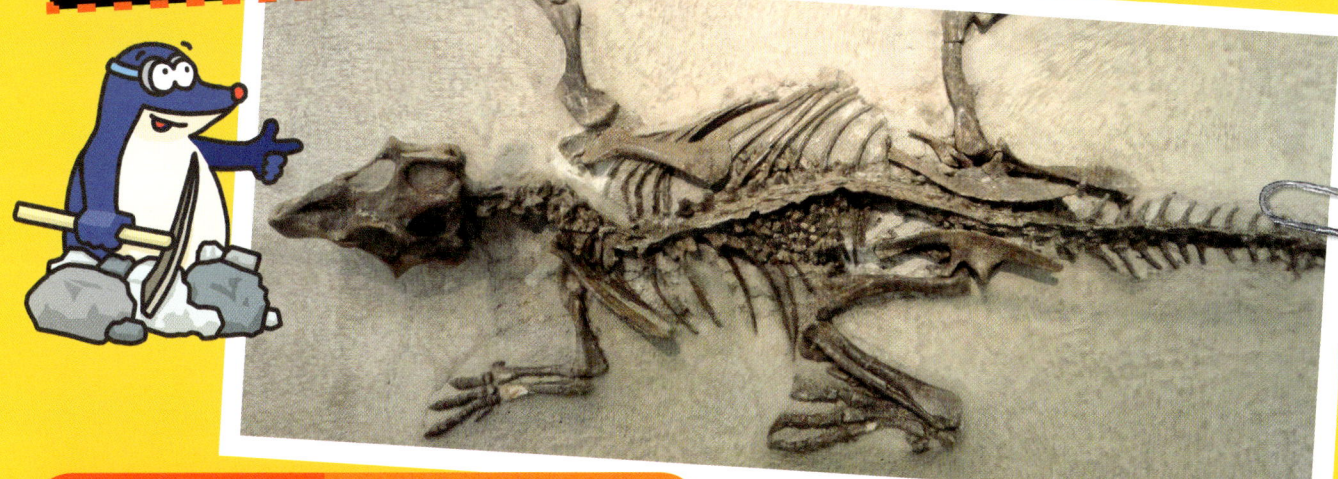

The Geology:

Geologists need several pieces of **evidence** before they can be sure that a rock is a dinosaur gastrolith.

- The rock must be unlike other rocks nearby. This shows the dinosaur traveled to the area with the gastrolith in its stomach.
- The rock should be rounded and polished. A gastrolith would have rubbed against other stones and material and become smooth.
- The stone must be found with or near the fossil of the dinosaur that swallowed it.

Asking the Questions

Study the photograph of the dinosaur fossil above.

- Can you see any rocks that might be gastroliths?
- Are they in or near the skeleton of the dinosaur?
- Are they in or near where the stomach might have been?
- Are there any rocks that look similar nearby?
- If you can see gastroliths, are they smooth and rounded?

Where Can You Find Fossils?

To have a chance of finding fossils, you need to find the right kind of rock. Most fossils are found in sedimentary rock. Fossil hunters look for areas of sedimentary rock that have either risen to the surface, or where the surrounding rock has worn away. Sedimentary rock is usually formed in water, so some of the best places to look are near water, where water used to be, or where rock has been worn away.

Useful things to have when fossil hunting
- Toilet paper to wrap any fossils in
- Food bags and a backpack to carry them home
- A small shovel, geology hammer, chisel, and eye protection
- A field journal and pen for recording your finds
- Plenty of water
- A phone in case you get into difficulty

Do

Only fossil hunt where it is okay to collect fossils. Check with an adult if you're not sure.

Stay away from cliff edges.

Keep an eye on the tides.

Beware of sinking sand or mud.

Wear eye protection in case rock fragments hit your face.

If you find a really interesting fossil, leave it, note where it is, and let a museum know.

Don't

Never go fossil hunting alone.

Don't climb or wander into dangerous areas.

Never touch unknown animals – they might be poisonous.

Don't hammer at cliffs – it can cause a rockfall.

Don't try to take large fossils. Photograph them instead, so others can enjoy them too.

HANDS-ON Planning a Fossil Hunt

You will need:
- access to a computer
- maps of the area

adult help needed

Remember – Never fossil hunt alone. Decide where would be the best place to search, and tell someone where you're going before your group sets off.

Visit local museums and visitor centers, or search for local fossil hunter clubs or rock shops. These places will help you learn which fossils are common in the area, so you can recognize any fossils you might find. Ask an adult to help you search the internet for information on local fossils. Look at maps of the area. **Geological maps** will show you where each different type of rock can be found.

BE A PALEONTOLOGIST
Keeping a Fossil Hunt Field Journal

You Will Need:
- a notebook
- a pencil

How to Keep Records:
It is easy to forget the details of a find once you get home. Make sure you have your journal with you on your fossil hunt. Note all the facts about your discovery.

The Geology:
Fossil hunters note details of their finds. It is important to record things like the kind of rock the fossil was found in, how deep underground the fossil was, and if there were any other fossils nearby. This may help paleontologists work out where and when the animal lived, what it ate, and how it died.

Date: July 27th, 2021, early morning
Fossil hunters: Ian and Rebecca
Place: Linton Marshes
Find: ammonite
Special comments: The ammonite was on the surface of a steep slope, in a layer of what looked like limestone. The rock was soft and broke away easily.

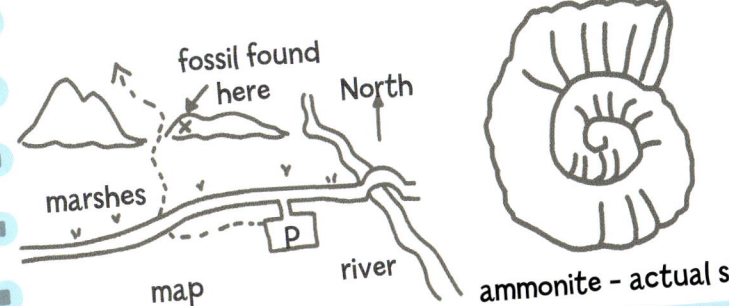

17

How the Experts Dig Up Fossils

As fossilization is rare, each fossil can hold vital information about prehistoric times. If you find an interesting fossil, especially an animal fossil, contact a museum for help before you try to excavate it. Why? There are many reasons why it is often better NOT to excavate a fossil:

- It's easy to damage a fossil during excavation. You may lose the information it could have provided.
- Removing a fossil takes it away from its **context**. Context is the fossil's surroundings, which give paleontologists information about where it lived, what it ate, and what other species were around at the same time.
- You might find bones of several animals. Leaving the fossils in place makes it easier for an expert to tell which bones belong to which animal.

Paleontologists will make notes and draw sketches of the site.

These are some of the tools a paleontologist might take to a dig.

brushes and dental picks

a geological hammer

a tape measure

Geological hammers have a flat face at one end for breaking rock. At the other end they either have a chisel or a pointed tip for cutting and picking out the rock.

HANDS-ON Try Excavating

It is useful to take photographs of the site at different stages of the excavation.

You will need:
- paintbrushes
- a toothpick
- a spoon
- eye protection
- gloves
- spray bottle
- some water

See if you can carefully excavate the mold and cast fossil you made on page 9. Imagine the surrounding material is the sedimentary rock at your excavation site. To take the fossil back to your museum, you are going to have to carefully brush and pick away the surrounding rock. Can you manage to do it without breaking your fossil?

Try spraying the surrounding rock with water and then gradually pick and brush it away using your tools.

fossil

surrounding rock

Fossils can be so brittle they would shatter if you tried to remove them. Paleontologists soak the bone in a thin glue. Once dry, this holds the fossil together enough to let them remove it.

Paleontologists use paintbrushes and dental picks to slowly remove the surrounding rock. They might soften the sediment by lightly spraying it with water.

Fossil Identification

How do you know if you have found a fossil? If the area you found your specimen in is known for fossils, there is a chance your specimen might be one. Fossils, like this dinosaur bone pictured, are usually a different color and smoother than the surrounding rock.

If paleontologists think they've found a dinosaur bone, they might lick it! Fossil bones have tiny holes which cause them to stick to the tongue slightly. But don't you try it!

Some common fossils:

Ammonite

Ammonite mollusks lived in the sea and are one of the most common fossils. They have spiral shells, usually with ridges. There were more than 10,000 species of ammonites!

Brachiopods

Brachiopods are marine animals that still exist today. Their fossilized shells can be brown, gray, black, or white depending on the rock they are preserved in.

Corals

Corals are related to jellyfish and anemones and most live in warm, shallow seas. Finding coral fossils shows us the area must once have been a warm sea.

Crinoids

Crinoids are related to starfish and appeared in the seas about 300 million years before dinosaurs! They look a little like flowers with ridged stems.

Echinoids

Echinoids are sea urchins. They have lived in the seas for 450 million years. Echinoids' long spine fossils are found more often than their brittle shells.

Trilobites

Trilobites are buglike creatures. Their name means "three lobes," as their bodies are divided into three parts. They became extinct about 250 million years ago.

BE A PALEONTOLOGIST
What Can a Fossil Skeleton Tell You?

Examining a Skeleton

Write down everything you know about chickens. You might say they have beaks and wings, eat worms, are covered in feathers, and walk on two legs. Look at the drawing of the chicken skeleton on the right. How many of those things can you tell from the skeleton alone?

Look at the dinosaur skeleton drawing, below. Can you answer these questions just by looking at the skeleton?
- Did it eat meat or plants?
- Do you think it could run fast?
- Did it walk on two or four legs?
- Do you think it had a large brain?

Which type of dinosaur do you think it is?

The Geology:

Paleontologists can tell a lot about a dinosaur from its skeleton. This dinosaur's sharp teeth show it mostly ate meat. Strong back legs hint that it could run fast. It probably used its short front legs for holding prey. The skull size hints it had quite a large brain. But—the skeleton can't show if it was covered in feathers, what color it was, or if it had scales.

Think About This...

Can you see similarities between the chicken and *Tyrannosaurus rex* skeleton?

Travel Through Time

When was the first sign of life on Earth? How long ago did dinosaurs wander on our planet? When did the first humans live? To help answer these questions, paleontologists use a time scale known as **geologic time**. Geologic time is like a calendar of Earth's geologic history since it began. Geologic time starts around 4 **billion** years ago, when Earth's crust was formed. How do we know it was formed then? The very oldest rock that geologists have found is about 4 billion years old.

BE A PALEONTOLOGIST
Make a Geologic Timeline Clock

You Will Need:
- a plate to draw around
- paper
- scissors
- a pencil and ruler
- colored pencils

The Geology:

The only life-forms that existed in the whole of the Precambrian **era** were bacteria, jellyfish, and algae! Most of the fossils that we find are from the more recent Paleozoic, Mesozoic, and Cenozoic eras. The chart on the next page shows all the creatures that lived during these later eras.

How to Keep Records

If you imagine all of geologic time was compressed into just 12 hours, this geological clock shows how long each era lasted. Draw around a plate on a piece of paper. Cut out the circle. Fold it in half, and then into quarters. Open it out. Write the 3, 6, 9, and 12 on your clock at the folds. Then add the other numbers. Draw lines from the center of the circle to the points of the clock, as shown. Now color and label your timeline.

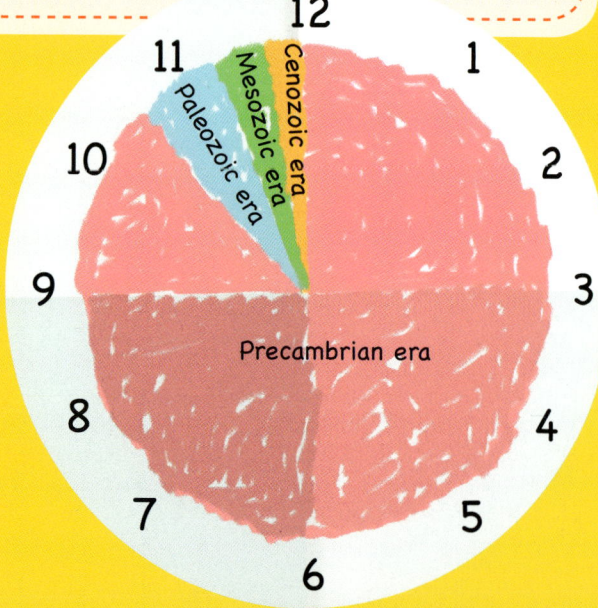

This geologic timeline shows the fossils we might find from the four main eras. The eras are divided into periods. "MYA" stands for "millions of years ago."

MYA	Era	Period
0	Cenozoic	**Quaternary** — Rise of humans
1.8	Cenozoic	**Tertiary** — Rise of mammals
50		
100	Mesozoic	**Cretaceous** — Modern seed-bearing plants, dinosaurs
150	Mesozoic	**Jurassic** — First birds
200		
250	Mesozoic	**Triassic** — First dinosaurs
300	Paleozoic	**Permian** — First reptiles
	Paleozoic (Carboniferous)	**Pennsylvanian** — First insects
350	Paleozoic (Carboniferous)	**Mississippian** — Many crinoids
400	Paleozoic	**Devonian** — First sea plants, cartilaginous fish
450	Paleozoic	**Silurian** — Earliest land animals
500	Paleozoic	**Ordovician** — Early bony fish
550	Paleozoic	**Cambrian** — Invertebrate animals, brachiopods, trilobites
2500	Precambrian	Bacteria, algae, jellyfish
4000	Precambrian	Earth's crust cools and continents and life start to form.
4540	Precambrian	Formation of Earth

How Old Is My Fossil?

Dating fossils is not easy. There are three main methods scientists use. They either work out how old the rock layer the fossil was found in is, study materials in the fossil itself using methods such as **carbon dating**, or study magnetic minerals in the rocks. Earth's magnetic field has changed through time and this can leave clues to a fossil's age.

Carbon and Uranium

A type of carbon in all living things decays at a particular rate once something dies. Scientists work out how long ago an animal died by examining the fossil's carbon. Some **elements** such as **uranium** are **radioactive**. Over time, they become less radioactive. Paleontologists can measure this decay in any uranium-containing rock to work out how old a fossil is.

If a fossil is found in a dark cave, a special meter can show paleontologists when the buried sediment last saw daylight.

Think About This...

Fossils do not occur in rock that contains uranium. How does knowing how old that rock is help date the fossil layers?

HANDS-ON Dating Things Using Layers
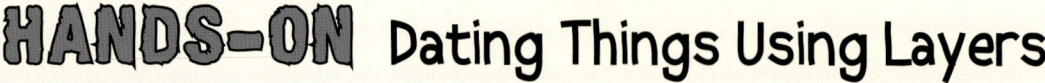

You will need:
- a pencil
- some paper
- a laundry basket

Ask your family to not do laundry for a week. Write the days of the week on pieces of paper. On Monday, hide the Monday note in the clothes you put in the laundry. Do the same for each day of the week. On Sunday, amaze your family by telling them what they wore each day. Use the hidden notes in your layers as clues. Remember to take the notes out, so they don't end up in the wash!

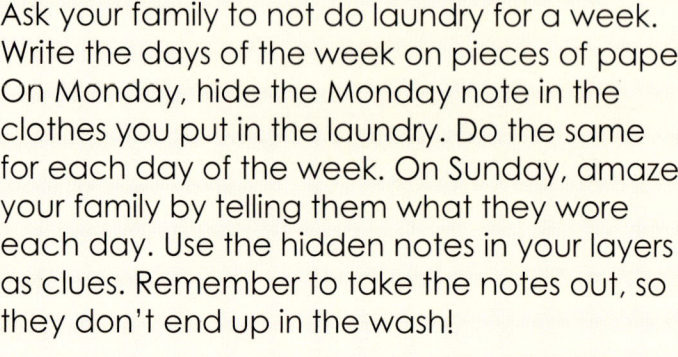

24

If paleontologists can't easily date a rock layer, they try to find other fossils in the same layer that can help them. Known as index fossils, certain fossils were only alive at a particular period. Finding an index fossil near the fossil they want to date is very helpful. Ammonites and trilobites make good index fossils because they are common, and different species lived during distinct time periods. Can you see the different patterns in the shells of the ammonite fossils below?

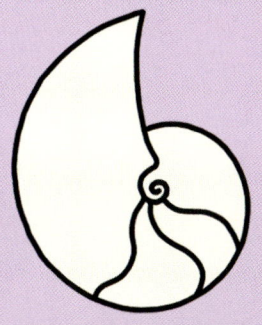  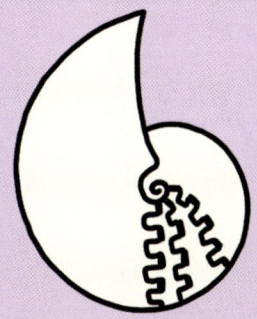 

BE A PALEONTOLOGIST
Date a Dinosaur Using Index Fossils

You Will Need:
- a deep container
- soil
- paper and pen
- scissors
- four plastic dinosaurs
- some tape
- a friend

Asking the Questions

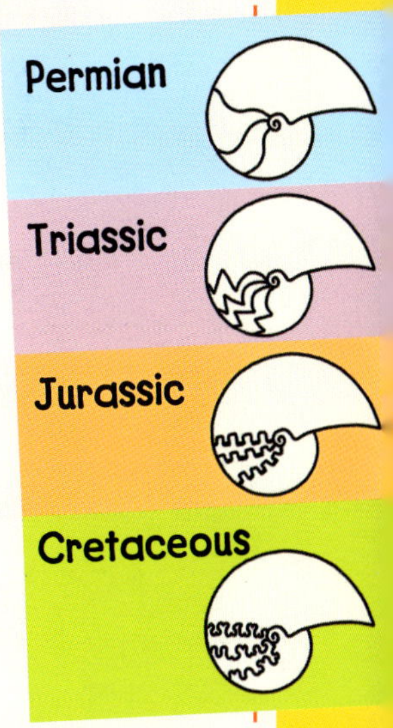

Design four ammonites. You could copy the ones pictured above. Draw each one on a separate piece of paper. Tape one ammonite to each plastic dinosaur. Decide what time period each ammonite lived in. Make a chart with a picture of each ammonite next to its time period.

Put some soil in the bottom of your container. Put the oldest dinosaur and ammonite in the soil. Then add a second layer of soil, and the next oldest dinosaur and ammonite. Repeat until you have buried all four. Ask a friend to excavate the dinosaurs. Can they work out how old they are using your chart?

Permian

Triassic

Jurassic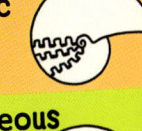

Cretaceous

The Geology:

Ammonite shells have chambers that join at places called sutures. The shell suture pattern tended to get more complicated over time. So the less wiggly the sutures on an ammonite fossil are, the older the fossil probably is.

25

Using Maps to Help Find Fossils

Before setting out on a fossil-hunting expedition, paleontologists will usually look at a geological map. A geological map shows the age and type of rocks in an area. Studying a map first means they will not waste time looking in areas with the wrong rock. Fossil hunters don't just look for a particular type of rock. The rock also needs to be the right age for the fossils they are looking for.

Most fossils are found in sedimentary rock. Dinosaur fossils are found in sedimentary rock that was formed in the Mesozoic era.

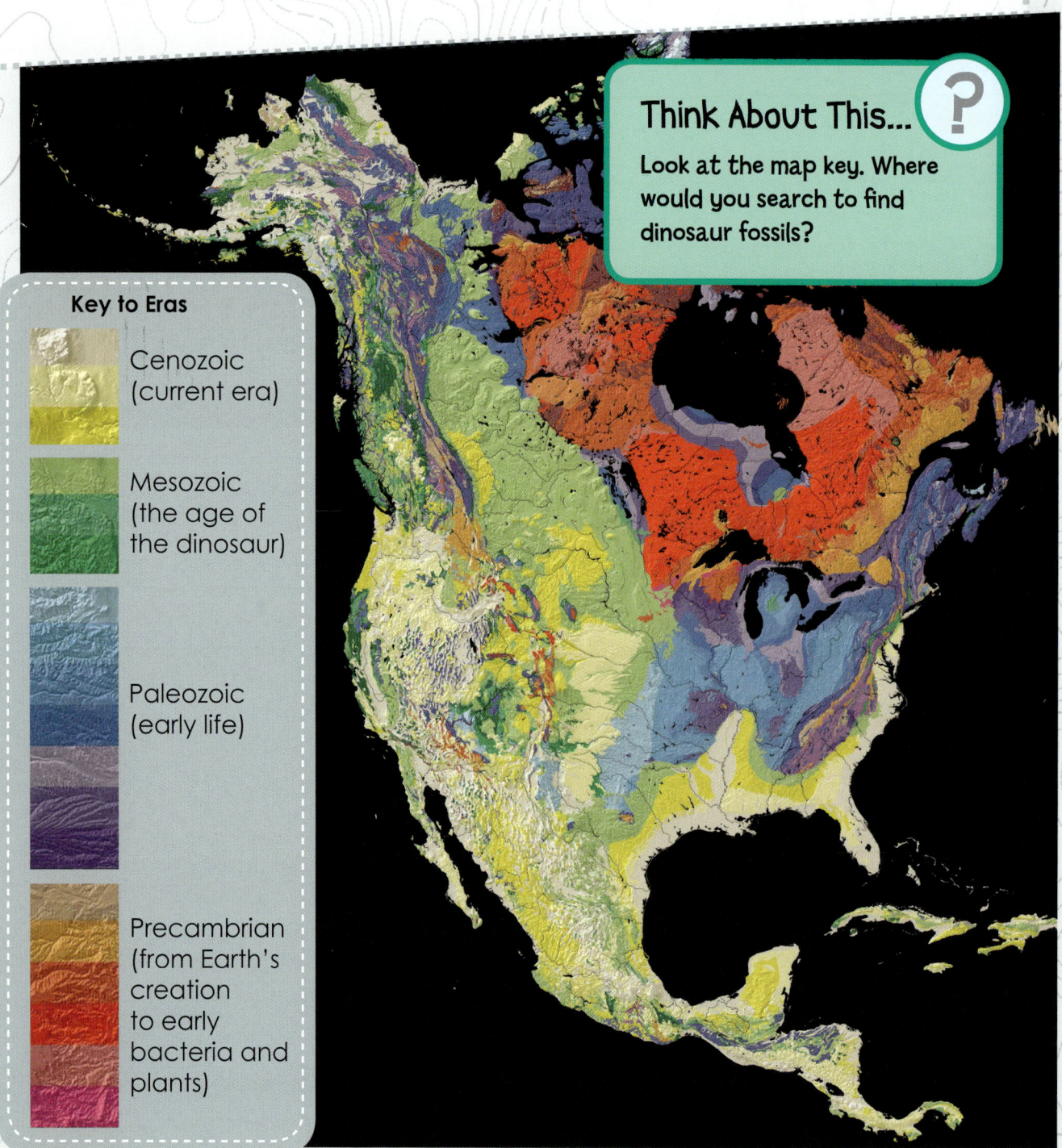

Think About This...

Look at the map key. Where would you search to find dinosaur fossils?

Key to Eras

Cenozoic (current era)

Mesozoic (the age of the dinosaur)

Paleozoic (early life)

Precambrian (from Earth's creation to early bacteria and plants)

BE A PALEONTOLOGIST
Make a Geological Map of Your Area

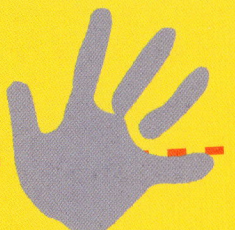

You Will Need:

- paper
- colored pencils or crayons
- greaseproof or tracing paper
- some tape
- a ruler

The Geology:

Mapmakers use aerial photographs and surveys to create their base maps. They find out how old the rock is in the same way as they age fossils.

If you want to find *Tyrannosaurus rex* fossils, look for exposed rock around 65 million years old. If you want to find a trilobite, you need even older rock, more than 245 million years old. Once you find the right rock, finding a fossil still needs a bit of luck, too.

How to Make Your Map:

Make a basic outline of the area you want to map. Perhaps draw your yard or street. Tape a sheet of tracing paper along one edge, so it flaps over your drawing. Draw a grid on this layer, dividing your map into squares. Try to get each square of your map around a pace apart in real life.

With your map as reference, go to each area of your grid. Dig up a tiny bit of soil. What is it like? Can you roll it into a ball? Then it is probably clay. Is it gritty like sand? Or is it dark with woody bits like compost? Perhaps you found large areas of gray solid rock, or small pebbles, or lighter, sandy rock? Look up some information on rocks and see if you can identify them.

Make a key for your map. Give each soil or rock type a different color. Mark each grid square with the correct color spots.

Key
- gray rock
- sandy rock
- pebbles
- normal soil
- rich compost
- clay soil

North

scale: 1 square = 1 pace

Sharing the Knowledge

You can find information about fossils at some local museums. They may have local area geological maps and examples of fossils that have been found in your area too. In areas well known for fossils, there are often groups where people with an interest in fossils meet and give talks. They may be happy to help you identify fossils that you find too.

To stay safe, make sure you ask your parents or caregivers to help you contact a group, and to come along with you.

BE A PALEONTOLOGIST
Make Your Own Fossil Exhibit

You Will Need:

- some fossils
- paper and pen
- information leaflets
- a table
- some wall space
- the projects you made in this book

Setting Up Your Display

It's fun to create your own museum display. Gather together any fossils that you have and place them on a table. You could display them in boxes if they are very small. Put labels next to each fossil with as much information as you can. You could put where you found or bought it, what you think it might be, and how old you think it is.

MORE IDEAS - Make some posters to go on the wall that tell visitors all about fossils. Put out any tools that you used to excavate them. You could try drawing some dinosaurs and other ancient animals too. Display your geological map and trace fossil, if you made them. Challenge visitors to date fossils using your index ammonites.

This way to the Fossil Museum

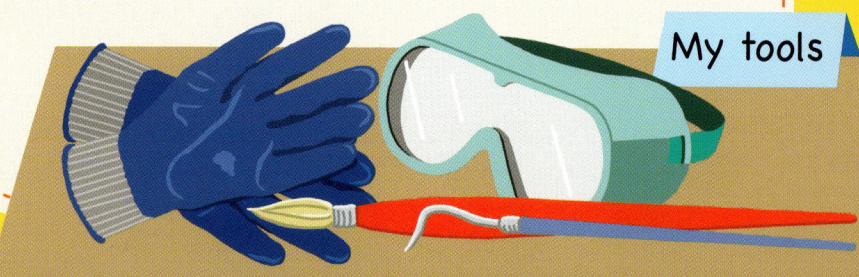

My tools

HANDS-ON Create a Dinosaur Landscape

You will need:
- a large tray or bowl
- some toy dinosaurs
- some small plants
- soil or sand
- rocks and pebbles

Create your own model of a prehistoric scene. Put a layer of sand or soil into a tray. Place some rocks and pebbles around your landscape. Push some small plants into the soil. Add your toy dinosaurs. You could display your model in your museum.

Why not photocopy a dinosaur skeleton and ask visitors to design what it might have looked like. What color was it? Did it have skin, hair, scales, or feathers?

Make some tickets to hand out at the door. You could write a small guide explaining your exhibits and give visitors the guide when they arrive. Maybe make a quiz for visitors to take to see if they have learned anything from your exhibits! Once you are all set up, invite your friends and family to come and visit your museum.

The Geology:

It's great to share knowledge with other fossil hunters. Everyone can learn from everyone else. Because some fossils are quite rare, it is important to share the ones you have found. They could hold important information that no one has ever found before!

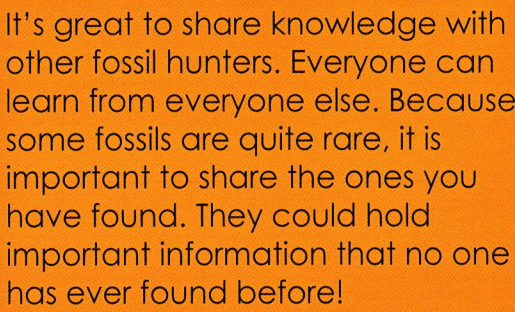

Model fossils

Glossary

bacteria single-celled microorganisms that live in soil, water, and the bodies of plants and animals.

billion a thousand million, written 1,000,000,000.

carbon dating the measurement of age (as of a fossil) by means of the amount of carbon-14 in the material.

cementation when minerals crystallize in the spaces between particles and hold them tightly together.

cemented united by or as if by cement.

compacted made or became compact.

compaction when loose particles in sediment are squashed until there is little or no empty space left between each particle.

compounds substances formed by the union of two or more chemical elements.

compressed reduced the size, amount, or volume by pressure.

context the setting for an event, idea, or statement by which it can be fully understood.

continents the great divisions of land on the globe.

coprolite fossilized poop.

decompose to break down an organism through biological activity (for example, by bacteria) into simpler chemical substances.

elements fundamental substances that consist of atoms of only one kind and that cannot be separated into simpler substances.

era one of the five major divisions of geologic time.

evidence available facts or information indicating whether a belief is true.

extinct no longer existing.

gastroliths small stones swallowed by a bird, reptile, or fish to aid digestion.

geological maps special-purpose maps made to show various geological features.

geologic time the long period of time occupied by Earth's geologic history.

groundwater the water found underground in the cracks and spaces in soil, sand, and rock.

lithification the process by which materials are converted into solid rock, as by compaction or cementation.

minerals solid chemical compounds that occur naturally in the form of crystals.

paleontologists scientists who study fossils.

paraffin a soft, colorless solid derived from petroleum, coal, or shale oil.

petrified converted into stone through a slow process of mineralization.

radioactive having or producing the energy that comes from the breaking up of atoms.

replica an exact copy of an object.

resin a sticky yellow or brownish substance obtained from the gum or sap of some trees.

sediment material such as stones and sand deposited by water, wind, or glaciers.

sedimentary rock rock formed by or from sediment.

uranium a chemical element that is a dense, gray, radioactive metal used as a fuel in nuclear reactors.

volcanic relating to or produced by a volcano.

Further Information

Museums and Places to Visit

Visit a museum. Most big city museums will have some fossil exhibits, workshops, and information about local finds.

Visit local rock shops. You can usually find some interesting fossils to look at or buy.

Look for fossil-hunting clubs or groups. Some areas, especially areas that are well known for fossils, will have clubs or groups you can join.

Useful Websites

This OneGeology site has all kinds of information about fossils and dinosaurs.
http://www.onegeology.org/extra/kids/fossils.html

The Natural History Museum features a cartoon showing how fossils are formed, and plenty of other great information too.
https://www.nhm.ac.uk/discover/how-are-fossils-formed.html

The American Museum of Natural History website is packed with facts about fossils.
https://www.amnh.org/dinosaurs/dinosaur-facts

Books to Read

Lynch, Dan R. *Fossils for Kids: Finding, Identifying, and Collecting.* Cambridge, MA: Adventure Publications, 2020.

Morgan, Ben. *Eyewitness Explorer: Rock and Fossil Hunter: Explore Nature with Loads of Fun Activities.* New York, NY: DK Children, 2015.

Publisher's note to parents and teachers: Our editors have reviewed the websites listed here to make sure they're suitable for students. However, websites may change frequently. Please note that students should always be supervised when they access the internet.

Index

algae 22, 23
amber 12
ammonite 4, 17, 20, 25
animals 4, 6, 7, 8, 9, 10, 12, 13, 16, 18, 24, 28

bacteria 12, 13, 22, 23, 26
birds 7, 13
body fossils 6
bones 6, 8, 12, 13, 14, 16, 20
brachiopods 20, 23
burrows 7

calcium carbonate 11
Cambrian period 23
carbon 24
carbon dating 24
Carboniferous period 23
cementation 11
Cenozoic era 22, 23, 26
chemicals 11
claws 6
clay 9, 12, 13, 27
compaction 4, 8, 9, 11
context 18
continents 5, 23
copper 14
coprolite 6
corals 20
Cretaceous period 5, 23, 25
crinoids 20, 23

dating fossils 24, 25
Devonian period 23
dinosaurs 4, 6, 7, 10, 14, 15, 20, 21, 22, 23, 25, 26, 28, 29

echinoids 20
eggs 6
elements 24
enamel 6
erosion 13
excavation 16, 18, 19

fish 8, 12, 23
footprints 7
fossil formation 4, 8
fossil hunting 16, 17, 26

gastroliths 15
geological maps 17, 26, 27, 28
geologic time 22
Gondwana 5
groundwater 11

humans 23

ice 12
identification 20, 21
index fossils 25
insects 7, 12, 13, 14, 23
iron 11, 14

jellyfish 22, 23
Jurassic period 5, 23, 25

Laurasia 5
lithification 10

magnetic field 24
mammals 23
manganese 14
Megalosaurus 6
Mesozoic era 22, 23, 26
minerals 8, 9, 10, 11, 14, 24
Mississippian period 23

mold and cast 8, 9
museums 17, 28, 29

Ordovician period 23

paleontologists 5, 12, 14, 17, 19, 20, 22, 24, 25, 26
Paleozoic era 22, 23, 26
Pangaea 5
peat 12
Pennsylvanian period 23
Permian period 5, 23, 25
Petrified National Forest, Arizona 14
petrified wood 14
plants 4, 7, 8, 10, 12, 13, 23, 26
Precambrian era 22, 23, 26

Quaternary period 23

radioactivity 24
reptiles 23
resin 12

safety 16
sand 11
sediment 4, 8, 9, 10, 11, 14, 24
sedimentary rock 4, 12, 16, 19, 26
shells 6, 20, 25
silica 11
Silurian period 23
sinking sand 16
skeletons 6, 8, 14, 15, 21, 29
skin 6
skulls 6
spider 12

teeth 6, 12, 13, 15
Tertiary period 23
tools 16, 18, 19, 28
trace fossils 6, 7, 28
trees 14
Triassic period 5, 23, 25
trilobites 20, 23, 25, 27
Tyrannosaurus rex 21, 27

uranium 24

volcanic ash 14

weather 13
whole body fossils 12, 13
wood 14
woolly mammoth 12